GYMNASTICS

GYMNASTICS

ART BERKE

A First Book   Franklin Watts
New York/London/Toronto/Sydney/1988

FRONTIS: KRISTIE PHILLIPS, THE CURRENT TOP
U.S. WOMEN'S GYMNAST, PERFORMS ON THE BALANCE BEAM.

Cover photograph by Dave Black

Diagrams by Anne Canevari Green.

Photographs courtesy of: Dave Black: pp. 2, 10, 18 (right), 25, 29,
36, 43, 52, 61, 65, 75, 79, 81 (top and bottom left, bottom right), 82,
83, 85 (top and bottom right); The Bettmann Archive, Inc.: p. 13;
Culver Pictures, Inc: p. 15; UPI/Bettmann Newsphotos: pp. 17 (top), 49,
81 (top right—Reuters); Sygma: p. 17 (bottom—Alain Dejean); United
States Gymnastic Federation: p. 18 (left—Rich Kinnsy); AAU: p. 33;
AP/Wide World Photos: p. 45, 69, 71, 81 (middle right), 85 (bottom left).

Library of Congress Cataloging-in-Publication Data

Berke, Art.
Gymnastics / Art Berke.
p.   cm. — (A First book)
Includes index.
Summary: Introduces the events, skills, and movements
of gymnastics and profiles individuals who have made outstanding
contributions in the field in the last two decades.
ISBN 0-531-10478-8
1. Gymnastics—Juvenile literature. 2. Gymnastics—United States—
Juvenile literature. 3. Gymnasts—Biography—Juvenile literature.
(1. Gymnastics. 2. Gymnasts.) I. Title.
GV461.B426 1988
796.4'1—dc19   87-23745 CIP AC

To Bonnie,
who has made my life a "Perfect 10"

CONTENTS

Introduction
11

Chapter I
Artistic Gymnastics
22

Chapter 2
Women's Events
28

Chapter 3
Men's Events
40

Chapter 4
Judging and Scoring
56

Chapter 5
Rhythmic Gymnastics
59

Chapter 6
How to Become a Gymnast
63

Chapter 7
The Greats of Gymnastics
67

Chapter 8
The 1988 Summer Olympics
77

Current USGF Member Organizations
87

Index
91

ACKNOWLEDGMENTS

The author would like to thank Kathy Kelly, Robert Cowan, Susan Polakoff, Jan Claire, Kathy Brown, and Jana Wilson of the U.S. Gymnastics Federation and ABC Sports commentator Gordon Maddux for their cooperation and guidance.

INTRODUCTION

The sport of gymnastics can take many forms. At its simplest, it is a cartwheel, a somersault, or playful tumbling and trampolining in the backyard. In its most sophisticated form, it is the events that comprise what we know today as competitive gymnastics.

Gymnastics is excellent exercise and a great deal of fun—precisely what the Greeks and Romans had in mind when they introduced the activity in ancient times. Competitive gymnastics, both the artistic (the more traditional) form and rhythmic varieties, go beyond that. Not only does the sport give a youngster a chance to compete and be the best, it also fosters many qualities that are vitally important in every aspect of life—qualities such as self-expression, coordination, discipline, confidence, pride of accomplishment,

U.S. gymnast Julianne McNamara performs in the 1984 Olympics in Los Angeles.

body awareness, the joy of physical activity, and the ability to get along with others.

Television coverage of and participation in the sport have grown by leaps and bounds during the past two decades. From the outstanding athletes who represent their countries in international competition to the millions of youngsters everywhere enrolled in gymnastics programs, the sport has never been so popular.

The purpose of this book is to introduce you to all aspects of gymnastics—the history, levels of competition, events, skills required, judging and scoring, great champions, and a look at what it takes to become a gymnast. Gymnastics can certainly be a worthwhile and rewarding activity, and one that may be perfect for you.

A BRIEF HISTORY

Outstanding gymnasts, like the ones we see in the Olympic Games, represent what competitive gymnastics is today. But the ancient forms of the sport, including everything from acrobatics and tumbling to contortionism, were quite different.

History tells us that all modern forms of gymnastics, as well as the sports of track and field, boxing, wrestling, and fencing, probably had their beginnings during the Greek and Roman empires, when great emphasis was put on physical fitness. The Greeks were great believers in the coordination of mind and body, and they built elaborate complexes known as *gymnasia* for physical education training. These centers became popular gathering places for young and old alike.

As a symbol of the importance they placed on physical activity, the Greeks began the ancient Olympic Games, a festival dedicated to the Greek god Zeus. The first games, which took place in 776 B.C., consisted only of a foot race.

The Greeks were great believers in physical education. Shown here is a gymnasium complex and racecourse in Sparta.

Before long, however, a variety of competitive activities were incorporated.

When the Romans conquered the Greeks, in the second century B.C., they adopted much of the Greek culture and preserved the emphasis on physical fitness. However, whereas the Greeks considered physical prowess to be an important element in a person's mental and intellectual development, the Romans saw athletics, including gymnastics, more as a way to keep their soldiers prepared for battle. It was not uncommon in those times to see soldiers mounting and dismounting a wooden horse in preparation for the next conflict. This wooden horse, of course, became the forerunner of the apparatus now used for the vault and pommel horse events in gymnastics.

With the decline of both the Greek and Roman empires, gymnastics and other forms of athletics fell by the wayside, except for the acrobatics and dance used by acting troupes. It wasn't until the eighteenth and nineteenth centuries that the pure form of the sport of gymnastics surfaced once again in Germany. The sport made its modern Olympic debut during the first games in 1896 in Athens, Greece, and has developed into one of the most popular events.

The rebirth of the movement was most influenced by Johann Guts Muths and Frederick Jahn. Johann Muths, a disciple of the Greek physician Galen (a leader of the gymnastics movement in ancient times), included Galen's and other landmark philosophies in his work entitled *Gymnastics for Youth.* Friedrich Jahn, considered the father of modern gymnastics, taught the sport to strengthen the youth of Germany. He also developed several gymnastic apparatus and organized the first outdoor gymnastics center, which became the model for the *Turnverein,* or gymnastics club.

From these two men, and others such as Adolf Spiess, who introduced gymnastics activity into the schools, and Pehr Henrik Ling of Sweden, who emphasized free expression more than the Germans did, the gospel spread throughout Europe. And when European gymnastics enthusiasts emigrated to the United States, they brought their interest and know-how along with them and set up organizations throughout the United States, including the German Turnverein (or Turner) and its Czechoslovakian counterpart, the Sokol. The Young Men's Christian Association (YMCA), which was founded in Britain in 1844, also put great emphasis on its gymnastics program.

GYMNASTICS IN
THE UNITED STATES

For many years, in international and Summer Olympic competition, the United States found itself far behind other countries in artistic gymnastics excellence, largely due to a gen-

Female gymnasts practice their routines in
late nineteenth-century San Francisco.

eral lack of emphasis on it at all levels. In the early years countries such as Germany, France, Switzerland, Austria, and Finland dominated. More recently it has been the Soviet Union, Rumania, Japan, and China.

American gymnastics began to make great strides during the 1970s, both in terms of mass participation and level of performance on the international scene. It is generally acknowledged that when Olga Korbut of the Soviet Union displayed her infectious smile and extraordinary skill in front of a worldwide television audience at the 1972 Olympics in Munich, Germany, the popularity of the sport surged in the United States. And by the time Rumania's Nadia Comaneci captivated audiences with her unprecedented succession of perfect scores of 10 at the 1976 Olympics, the United States and the world had truly caught the gymnastics bug.

Even before the TV exposure of Korbut and Comaneci, Cathy Rigby had attracted many to the sport with her exceptional talent, engaging personality, and charismatic style. In 1970 she became the first American to win a medal at the world championship level when she collected a silver on the balance beam.

Another U.S. milestone was reached at the 1976 games in Montreal when Peter Kormann became the first American gymnast since the 1932 Olympics to win an Olympic medal. His bronze medal, although not publicized as much as some of the accomplishments of his female counterparts, went a long way in setting the stage for the U.S. men's team to take its rightful place in the gymnastics world.

Others who made great contributions to the rise of U.S. gymnastics in the 1970s were Kurt Thomas, perhaps the finest American male gymnast thus far, and Marcia Frederick. In the 1978 world championships, Thomas became the first American world champion, with a gold in the floor exercise, and a day later Frederick won a gold medal on the women's uneven parallel bars.

Olympic champion gymnast Olga Korbut, from the USSR, performs a split on the balance beam.

Fourteen-year-old Rumanian gymnast Nadia Comaneci displays one of the gold medals she won in the 1976 Olympic Games.

Left: *gymnastics great Kurt Thomas.*
Right: *Mary Lou Retton performs in the floor
exercise event at the 1984 Olympics.*

The milestone successes by Rigby, Kormann, Thomas, Frederick, and others laid the foundation for the unprecedented team effort by U.S. gymnasts at the 1984 Olympics in Los Angeles, resulting in a gold medal for the men's team, a silver for the women's team, an all-around gold for Mary Lou Retton, and other medal-winning performances.

PARTICIPATION
IN COMPETITION

The ancient Greeks and Romans and the pioneers in the gymnastics movement in the eighteenth and nineteenth centuries certainly would be surprised at how widespread and organized the sport has become.

The Federation of International Gymnastics (FIG) serves as the governing body for the seventy-eight member nations around the world and was formed to bring under one jurisdiction all the different styles and philosophies of gymnastics that exist throughout the world. The FIG is responsible for worldwide gymnastics development, rules, regulations, judging standards, equipment standards, and the coordination of such international competitions as the World Cup, the world championships, and, of course, the Olympic Games. Each of the member countries follows the federation's rules and also has its own committees to interpret these rules as they relate to their own competitions.

The U.S. Gymnastics Federation (USGF) is the governing body in this country. It is made up of more than 166,000 members, including approximately 55,000 competitive gymnasts in more than twenty amateur associations, including colleges and high schools. According to the USGF, which also lists nearly 8,000 coaches, judges, and other professionals among its members, its job is "to do whatever is necessary to promote and develop the sport of gymnastics in the United States."

Among the organization's responsibilities are: selecting and training teams to compete around the globe; organizing gymnastics meets at all levels; providing educational and safety clinics, training camps, and seminars; and developing public relations and marketing programs.

To best understand how gymnastics operates in the United States, we can look at the USGF "pyramid of participation," which outlines the five levels of competition:

GRASS-ROOTS GYMNASTICS. This is the bottom rung of the pyramid (and the most populated), where the gymnast takes the first step, whether it's at the YMCA or YWCA, a local club, or in the schools.

JUNIOR OLYMPIC PROGRAM. This program has five classifications, and as the individual gets older and his or her abilities grow, there is advancement to higher levels. Classes IV and V are for beginners, Classes III and II are for the intermediate levels, and Class I is for the most outstanding gymnasts in this particular program.

NATIONAL ELITE PROGRAM. In order to reach this level, the gymnast must achieve certain standards at the Class I level in the Junior Olympic program. This competition requires superior skills. It is also at this level that the gymnast participates in national championship competitions. The winners comprise the U.S. national teams, both junior and senior.

JUNIOR NATIONAL TEAM. The gymnasts who reach this level are the best in the country in their age groups (13–18 for boys and 10–14 for girls) and compete internationally against other junior national teams.

SENIOR NATIONAL TEAM. This is the top level of American gymnasts. These extraordinary gymnasts compete for spots on the U.S. team for such prestigious events as the world championships and the Olympic Games.

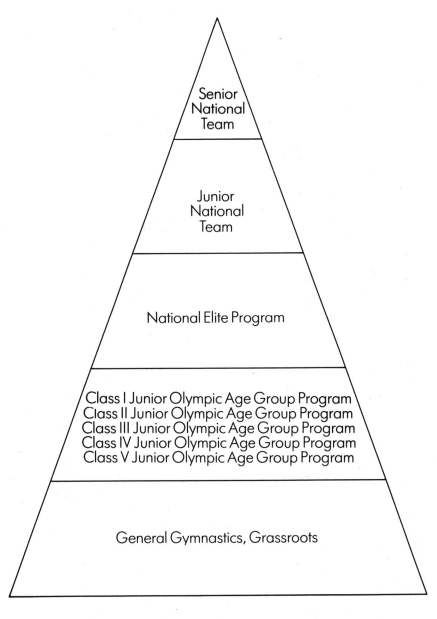

The Pyramid of Participation

1

ARTISTIC GYMNASTICS

The format of artistic gymnastics competition—which has undergone numerous changes over the years—currently consists of four events for women and six for men. Rhythmic gymnastics, which made its Olympic debut in 1984, will be discussed later in the book.

Female gymnasts compete in the vault, uneven parallel bars, balance beam, and floor exercise. The men perform in the floor exercise, pommel horse, rings, vault, parallel bars, and horizontal bar.

In addition to individual competition in these events, there are the all-around and team competitions. The all-around consists of the gymnast demonstrating his or her versatility by competing on all the apparatus and receiving one overall score. The gymnastics all-around is comparable to the decathlon event in track and field, and, as in track competition, the winner is usually considered the sport's finest athlete.

In Chapters 2 and 3 we will take a closer look at the current roster of events, for both men and women, in the order they are performed in most major meets. The selected routines show varying degrees of difficulty and consist of both compulsory (required) and optional (voluntary) moves.

Before we begin examining the various events, let's review some basic terms that are used in describing the events, skills, and movements in gymnastics.

ACROBATIC ELEMENTS—Movements such as saltos, handsprings, and twists, which come from tumbling skills. (See separate entries below on each of these movements.)

AMPLITUDE—The fullest extent of a particular movement.

ARCH—When the gymnast's back is curved outward.

BACKWARD ROLL—In this movement, the gymnast begins by squatting in a tucked position. The hands come up behind the body and the gymnast rolls backward, bringing the knees overhead. The hands are then placed on the mat under the shoulders, and the gymnast pushes with the arms as the legs pass over the head. The gymnast continues to push with the arms until his or her feet are on the ground and then follows through to a stand-up position.

BLIND RELEASE—A release movement (when a gymnast lets go of the apparatus) that causes the gymnast to lose sight of that apparatus during a routine.

BODY WAVE—A series of consecutive movements of different muscles of the body that become a single fluid movement.

BRIDGE—When the body is arched upwards with feet and hands on the floor.

CARTWHEEL—A common gymnastics exercise that is basically a handspring performed sideways.

CAST—An exercise on the horizontal bar or uneven parallel bars. It begins in the so-called front support position, with the body supported by the hands and the arms straight. The gymnast swings forward, then backward, all the while being supported only by the hands.

DISMOUNT (also called a LANDING)—A gymnast's last movement off an apparatus.

FLIP-FLOP (also called FLIC-FLAC)—A front or back handspring.

FORWARD ROLL—A basic movement performed the following way: The gymnast squats with knees together and hands on the floor in front of the knees. He or she pushes with both legs until they are straight, then bends the arms and lowers the head to the mat. The legs are brought into a tucked position, and the gymnast grabs the knees. He or she then rolls forward onto the feet, continuing to a squat and following through to a stand-up position.

GIANT SWING—A swinging motion with the body fully extended while making a complete revolution on the bars or rings.

GYMNASTIC ELEMENTS—Movements that include turns, jumps, leaps, hops, steps, and running combinations; balance skills in various positions; and arm swings and body waves.

*Kathy Johnson performs
in the 1984 Olympics.*

HANDSPRING—A jump where the body's weight is shifted from the feet to the hands with a thrust forward or backward.

HEADSPRING—The placing of the head between the hands on the floor, followed by a thrust while bringing the legs over to a squatting or standing position.

HIP CIRCLE—The circling of a gymnast's body around the horizontal bar or uneven parallel bars while keeping the hips in contact with the bar.

HURDLE—The step preparing a gymnast for a takeoff or a tumbling movement.

KIP—The movement of a gymnast from a hanging position to a support position on a bar apparatus.

LAYOUT—A position in which the body is straight and extended to its full length.

PIKE—A position in which the gymnast is bent at the waist with the legs and knees straight.

PIROUETTE—A movement during which the gymnast changes direction while being supported by the hands and arms and twists while in the handstand position.

ROUNDOFF—A version of the cartwheel. The main difference between the two is that this particular move contains a flight element (where the hands and feet are off of the ground).

SALTO—A flip or somersault without the use of the hands.

SQUAT—The bending of the knees and hips while remaining upright.

STICKING—This is when the gymnast completes the routine and lands without taking any additional steps.

STRADDLE—A position where the legs are held out straight and apart.

TUCK—A position where the knees are brought to the chest with the body folded at the waist.

TWIST—Turning movements that are defined by the amount the gymnast turns—full, one and a half, and so on.

VIRTUOSITY—A term used to describe the degree of excellence in a movement. The more fluidly a series of skills is performed, the greater the virtuosity and score.

WALKOVER—This exercise is performed both forward and backward. In the forward walkover, the gymnast moves from a standing position to a handstand, goes into a bridge position, and then goes back to a standing position. In the backward walkover, the gymnast slowly lowers backward to the hands, goes into the bridge position, then kicks to a handstand and lands on his or her feet.

2

WOMEN'S EVENTS

VAULT

The apparatus used for the women's vault, referred to as a horse, is 4 feet (1.2 m) high, 5 feet (1.5 m) long, and 14 inches (35 cm) wide. It is made of either wood or a combination of wood and steel. The body of the vault is padded, with either a leather or synthetic cover. The accompanying springboard is wood. The runway leading to the vault itself is 80 feet (24 m) long and 3 feet (1 m) wide.

The women's vault event requires speed, coordination, and timing. During the first phase of the vault, the gymnast sprints down a runway and takes a hurdle—a kind of skip-step— onto the springboard. She then propels herself onto the horse, which is placed perpendicular to the runway, and pushes off the horse toward the opposite side of the apparatus, performing her choice of any number of twists, somersaults, and cartwheel-type movements. The entire vault exercise lasts just a few seconds, from the initial sprint to the dismount or landing; therefore, the goal is to execute it as one fluid motion.

The sprint portion of the vault should provide the gymnast with the necessary momentum to make a strong push off the horse. Once the gymnast enters the support phase, that of pushing off the horse, she should be striving for proper position of body, shoulders, arms, and hands.

The key aspects of the next phase—flight from the horse and landing—are height and distance, plus the number and difficulty of half twists, full twists, and somersaults. The landing, which gives the spectators and judges a lasting impression of the entire exercise, should be clean and without extra movement, with the gymnast standing upright and the hands held straight above the head.

The women's vault

In Junior Olympic competition, the gymnast is given the opportunity to perform two different vaults, with the lowest score thrown out. In the finals of the Elite, which are the more advanced competitions, the gymnast must perform two different vaults, with the final score being an average of the two scores.

Naturally, vault routines vary in complexity. One example of a basic vault is the handspring, a routine in which the gymnast springs off the vault apparatus with a quick push from the hands. This is the essence of vaulting and must be mastered before learning other exercises. A more sophisticated handspring routine is the front handspring with a full turn (see Fig. 2.1).

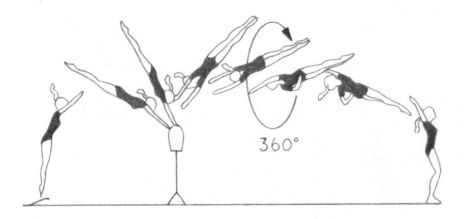

Fig. 2.1. Front Handspring with Full Turn

Among the most common vaults used in advanced optional competition are the different forms of the Tsukahara (named after the Japanese gymnast who first introduced the movement), one example being the Tsukahara per-

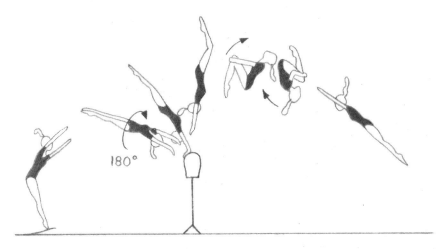

Fig. 2.2. Tsukahara Tucked

formed in the tuck position. The Tsukahara is basically a cartwheel onto the horse followed by a one-and-a-half back somersault (see Fig. 2.2).

UNEVEN PARALLEL BARS

The upper bar is 7.5 feet (2.3 m) high, the lower bar is 5 feet (1.5 m) high, and the apparatus is 8 feet (2.4 m) long. The bars are 1.7 inches by 2 inches (4.3 cm x 5 cm) wide and are usually made of wood with either steel, wood, or fiberglass uprights.

Of all four gymnastic events for women, the uneven bars is without question the most exciting for the spectator to watch and the most daring for the gymnast, who must display strength, concentration, balance, flexibility, and coordination as well as courage. While performing on the uneven bars, the gymnast moves from one bar to the other, incorpo-

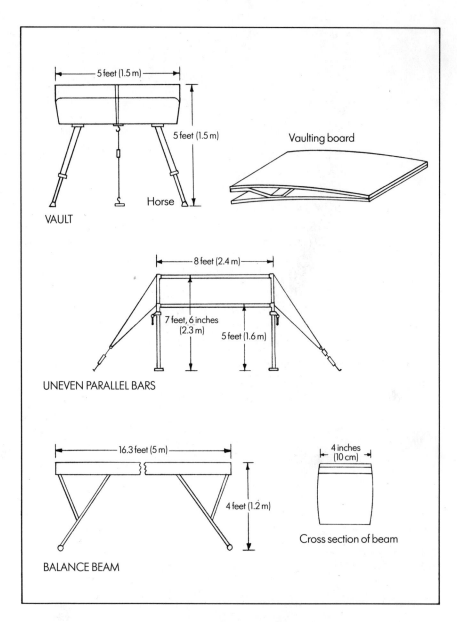

5 feet (1.5 m)

5 feet (1.5 m)

Vaulting board

Horse

VAULT

8 feet (2.4 m)

7 feet, 6 inches (2.3 m)

5 feet (1.6 m)

UNEVEN PARALLEL BARS

16.3 feet (5 m)

4 feet (1.2 m)

4 inches (10 cm)

Cross section of beam

BALANCE BEAM

Women's apparatus

rating a variety of movements and handgrips, keeping in mind that only four consecutive movements can be done on one bar.

The most exhilarating part of the uneven bars exercise for both participant and spectator is the coordination of kips, swings, circles, and saltos into one fluid motion. This motion includes the dismount, which should find the gymnast landing cleanly. An exceptionally creative dismount can mean a great deal to the entire exercise.

The putting together of such a routine, with all its varied movements, can be the ultimate in creative gymnastics. It allows for numerous innovations and techniques. Maximum amplitude and large swinging movements from and into a handstand will be viewed very favorably by the judges.

Performing on the uneven bars

A common move on the uneven bars is the cast. An example of a routine in which the cast is utilized is the cast movement to a handstand, with the legs spread apart and hips bent.

The clear hip circle is one of the basic swinging movements on the uneven bars. This routine begins with a cast movement and continues with a circle around a bar, with the gymnast holding her hips close to the bar (see Fig. 2.3).

Fig. 2.3. Clear Hip Circle to Handstand

A more advanced element that has become common in the past decade is the giant circle (or swing), a complete revolution of the straightened body from handstand to handstand. This has made the uneven bars more like the men's horizontal bar. An interesting aspect of the giant circle is that it has turned the uneven bars into an exercise of large circling movements. An example of a routine using this movement is the giant circle backward to a handstand with a half turn (see Fig. 2.4).

Fig. 2.4. Giant Circle Backward

BALANCE BEAM

The balance beam used in gymnastics competition is 4 inches (10 cm) wide, 4 feet (1.2 m) high, and 16.3 feet (5 m) in length. It is made of wood and covered by leather or synthetic padding. The steel bar is adjustable.

A gymnast performing on the balance beam can be one of the most graceful and aesthetically pleasing of all athletic sights, with many of the same movements utilized in the floor exercise. While competing on the beam, the gymnast must put together a routine of both acrobatic and gymnastic elements. This routine should last between 70 and 130 seconds and give the impression, by rhythm and flow, that the gymnast is performing on a much bigger surface. In fact, the nar-

The balance beam requires exceptional grace and strength.

row width of the balance beam makes it mandatory that the gymnast perfect her skills on a mat and floor-level beams before attempting the movements on the raised beam.

According to the official Code of Points issued by the Federation of International Gymnastics, the gymnast must perform the following: one acrobatic series; acrobatic movements in at least two directions; a series of gymnastic movements; a large gymnastic leap or jump; and a full turn on one leg.

It goes without saying that performing on the balance beam takes a great deal of self-confidence. The key is balance, but the gymnast must also be able to perform. She must gracefully bring together many different elements, such as walking, dancing, turning, and tumbling, in a smoothly flowing program. The dismount must be clean and confident and performed either off the side or at the end of the apparatus.

The forward and backward rolls, cartwheels, and forward and backward walkovers are basic balance beam movements. Naturally, the more daring routines on the beam (including the dismount) happen in the air. One of the most commonly used beam routines is the aerial walkover. This is a difficult skill made more difficult by the fact that the gymnast generally cannot see the beam during the landing (see Fig. 2.5).

Fig. 2.5. Aerial Walkover

FLOOR EXERCISE

The padded mat used in the floor exercise is 40 feet by 40 feet (12 m x 12 m).

The floor exercise routine is a combination of gymnastics, acrobatic, and dance movements. It is the most natural of all the events in that it is free of any supporting apparatus.

Fig. 2.6. Aerial Cartwheel

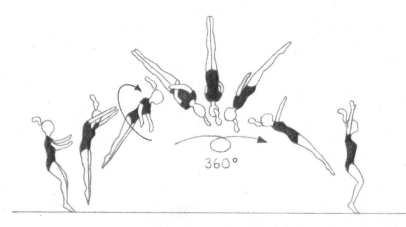

360°

Fig. 2.7. Salto Forward with Full Twist

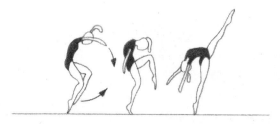

Fig. 2.8. Body Wave

In the floor exercise, the gymnast performs a 70- to 130-second routine set to music, utilizing the entire mat area. The key to a successful routine is for the competitor to find the right blend of tumbling, dancing, and acrobatic maneuvers, one especially suited to her own body and physical abilities. In the optional phase of this event, the music and choreography is chosen to suit the personality and skill level of the gymnast. This routine must also incorporate the required moves as determined by the Federation of International Gymnastics. And, like all of the other events we have discussed, the floor exercise movements must be performed fluidly, giving the impression that the routine is one continuous movement.

Perhaps the most distinctive aspect of the floor exercise is the chance for the gymnast to express her own unique personality, both artistically and athletically. It is also the final event performed in a meet. Therefore, it can be the climactic finish to a closely contested competition.

The movements performed during the floor exercise event range from the very basic ones such as the forward and backward rolls, cartwheels, roundoffs, handstands, flip-flops, and headsprings to the more delicate dancelike movements. Three tumbling series are required in the floor exercise, each containing a salto. Among the most popular floor exercise movements are the aerial cartwheel, a cartwheel movement performed with the gymnast in the air; and a forward salto with a full twist, which is a forward somersault flowing into a full twist of the body before landing on the feet (see Figs. 2.6 and 2.7).

3

MEN'S EVENTS

FLOOR EXERCISE

The padded mat in this event is 40 feet by 40 feet (12 m x 12 m).

The men's floor exercise routine is similar to the women's version, although the requirements are somewhat different and the men don't perform to music. The duration of the men's floor exercise routine is between fifty and seventy seconds. During that period the gymnast must perform a series of tumbling routines. These should demonstrate a combination of strength, flexibility, and balance over the entire surface of the mat. The transitions between the tumbling moves, gymnastic moves (turns, leaps, jumps, hops, etc.), and acrobatic moves (saltos, handsprings, twists, etc.) must be done smoothly and in one continuous motion.

A successful floor exercise routine consists of a demonstration of fundamental skills as well as elements with a high degree of difficulty. These include multiple saltos and twists with substantial height and clean landings.

There are a wide variety of movements with varying degrees of difficulty in the men's floor exercise routines. Examples are a jump forward to a handstand; leg circles, which are leg movements performed while the gymnast balances himself with his arms; and a tucked salto forward to a stand (standing position). This is a somersault in the tucked position before a landing on the feet (see Figs. 3.1, 3.2, and 3.3).

Fig. 3.1. Jump Forward to a Handstand

Fig. 3.2. Leg Circles

Fig. 3.3. Tucked Salto Forward to a Stand

Fig. 3.4. Press to a Handstand with Straight Legs

POMMEL HORSE

The pommel horse is 14 inches (35 cm) wide, 4 feet (1.2 m) high, and 5 feet (1.5 m) long. The body is made of either wood or a wood/steel material with the horse covered by leather or synthetic fabric. The pommels, or raised handles, can be made of wood or synthetic material.

While on the pommel horse, the gymnast relies mostly on his hands, the only part of the body that can be in contact with the apparatus. With the hands working back and forth on both pommels, the gymnast must make a series of circular motions with his legs while covering all three sections of the pommel horse—the middle portion and both ends. Vital to

A scissors routine on the pommel horse

the overall success of the routine, the legs should be straight with toes pointed. Each movement should flow into the next and appear to be effortless.

Two major factors contribute to the difficulty of the pommel horse. These are (1) that the skills used are different from the basic tumbling and swinging moves used in other events, and (2) that the gymnast must depend totally on the strength of one hand while the other prepares for the next move. The gymnast will frequently prepare for his dismount by performing handstands and twisting and circling movements.

Fig. 3.6. Backward Scissors

Fig. 3.5. Forward Scissors

Ever since gymnastics great Kurt Thomas introduced his "Thomas flair" routine, which features a whirling leg motion, this event has been one of the most innovative in the sport. Among the elements recently brought to the pommel horse is the handstand, once totally unrelated to the event.

One of the very first pommel horse skills taught to youngsters is known as the scissors. This is performed with both forward and backward leg movements. When the body is leaning forward, it is a front scissor (see Fig. 3.5). When the body is leaning backward, it is a back scissor (see Fig. 3.6). Another scissors routine is the scissors forward to a handstand.

RINGS

Two rings are used in this event. Each is 1.2 inches (2.8 cm) wide, 8 inches (20 cm) in diameter, 8.5 feet (2.6 m) off the mat surface, and suspended 18 feet (5.5 m) from a horizontal bar.

The rings require great upper body strength. Here Tom Schlesinger shows winning form in a 1987 U.S. men's competition.

Fig. 3.7. Cross

Upper body strength is the key to mastering the "still" rings, called that due to the importance of having these apparatus move as little as possible during the routine. The need for exceptional strength in the upper torso is evident when the gymnast performs the required movements demonstrating strength and agility. This includes at least two handstands. While performing the strength elements, such as a cross—when the body forms a crosslike position (see Fig. 3.7), the gymnast must stop for a full two seconds before moving on to the next task.

A skill learned by all beginning gymnasts is the back lever, which requires strength and balance (see Fig. 3.8). The planche is another routine that requires these elements. In it, the gymnast's body is parallel to the floor, supported by straight arms and hands on the apparatus (see Fig. 3.9). Among the common dismounts for the rings event are the use of front and back somersaults.

Perhaps the most exciting movement is the giant swing. This is when the gymnast, from a handstand position, swings through until he is once again in the handstand (see Fig. 3.10).

Fig. 3.8. Back Lever

Fig. 3.9. Planche

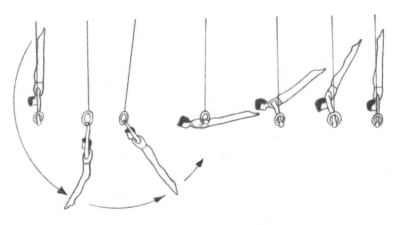

Fig. 3.10. Giant Swing Forward

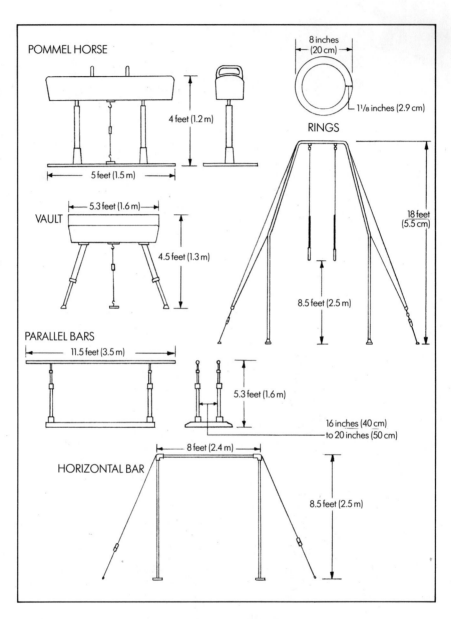

Men's apparatus

VAULT

The men's vault apparatus is 14 inches (35 cm) wide, 5.3 feet (1.6 m) long, and 4.5 feet (1.4 m) high. The body of the horse is made of either wood or wood and steel, with padding covered by leather or a synthetic material. The runway leading up to the vault is 82 feet (25 m) long and 3 feet (1 m) wide. The springboard is made of wood.

Although there are many similarities, the men's vault is quite different from the women's version of the event. Among the various differences are: the men vault over the length, instead of the width, of the apparatus; the men's horse is higher than the women's; and in most competitions the men vault only once, with that score going into the records.

Michel Boutard of France pushes himself off the horse vault in the 1984 Olympics.

As the gymnast sprints toward the apparatus on his initial approach, he must be concerned with getting enough acceleration. The proper speed will allow him to get the proper height and, in turn, get into the proper position for the next phase. The higher the flight and farther the distance traveled from the horse to the landing, the more successful the vault is judged. Movements such as saltos and twists are often utilized in the men's vault, but the time is so short in that final phase, from the push off the horse to the dismount, that it would be risky to get too fancy.

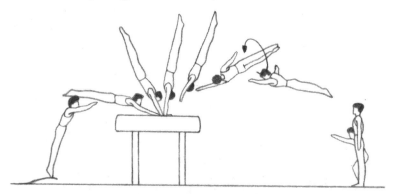

Fig. 3.11. Front Handspring with Half Turn

Fig. 3.12. Tsukahara Piked

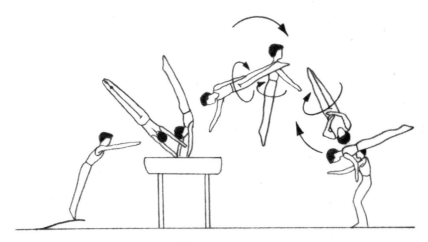

Fig. 3.13. Kasamatsu Stretched

Among the popular routines are: the front handspring with a half turn; the Tsukahara (basically a cartwheel onto the horse followed by a one-and-a-half back somersault) in the piked position; and the Kasamatsu performed in the layout position, which is basically a sideways handspring with an additional turn before the landing (see Fig. 3.13). Like the Tsukahara, the Kasamatsu routine is named after its originator.

PARALLEL BARS

The width of the parallel bars is adjustable from 16 inches (40 cm) to 20 inches (50 cm). The apparatus is 11.5 feet (3.5 m) in length and 5.3 feet (1.6 m) high. The diameter of the rails is 1.5 inches by 2 inches (3.75 cm x 5 cm). The bars are made of wood.

Also requiring a variety of skills, the parallel bars routine is a combination of swinging, holding, and flight elements. The

*U.S. men's
newcomer
Charlie Lakes
performs on the
horizontal bar.*

gymnast's objective is to swing smoothly while performing movements both above and below, and inside and outside, of the bars. Like the rings, this event takes great upper body strength. The top level of ''p-bar'' gymnasts perform daring stunts, utilizing different swinging elements to move into bold handstands and even losing sight of the apparatus with front and back saltos.

As in all events, the parallel bars require the gymnast to have rhythm and flow in the performance, climaxing with a high flight off the bars into a clean landing. The landing uses a combination of front and back somersault movements.

A basic routine in the p-bars is the underbar cast, usually a required movement that tests the gymnast's skills both above and below the bars (see Fig. 3.14). One advanced skill on the parallel bar apparatus is the Diamidov turn. This is a twisting swing forward that ends up in a handstand on one arm. (see Fig. 3.15). It was named after the Soviet gymnast who introduced it.

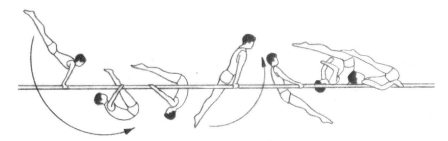

Fig. 3.14. Underbar Cast

Fig. 3.15. Diamidov Turn

HORIZONTAL BAR

The horizontal bar is 1.2 inches (2.8 cm) in diameter, 8.5 feet (2.6 m) high, and 8 feet (2.4 m) long. The bar is made of stainless steel.

Like the uneven bars for the women, the horizontal bar—which climaxes the men's program—provides the most exciting gymnastics for the spectator. It allows the gymnast to take considerable risk, both gymnastically and artistically.

The routine itself consists of continuous swinging movements including "giant swings." These utilize various handgrips and changes in body position and direction. A successful horizontal bar exercise demands that the gymnast be daring. For instance, he may choose a routine that uses swings with quick hand releases and then dismount with a variety of multiple saltos.

Among the more basic exercises on the horizontal bar are the cast (see Fig. 3.16) and hip circle movements. These are also performed on the women's uneven parallel bars (see Chapter 2).

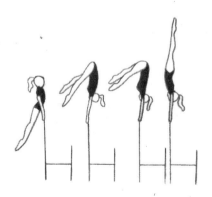

Fig. 3.16. Cast

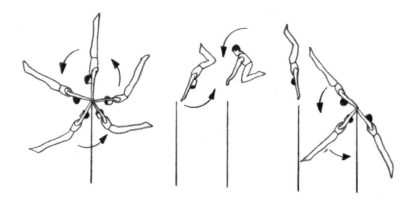

Fig. 3.17. Gaylord II

A movement made popular by an American gymnast of the same name, the Gaylord II is an excellent example of a risky move on the horizontal bar (see Fig. 3.17). The Gaylord II begins from a giant swing forward into a one-and-a-half forward salto (over the bar).

4

JUDGING
AND
SCORING

A gymnast in competition is evaluated by an established set of standards. The judging is a significant part of the competition process.

The set of criteria for each event is determined by the Federation of International Gymnastics and is written in the Code of Points. These rules cover every aspect of the gymnast's performance, including compulsory and optional skills.

In order to become a judge sanctioned by the international governing body, an individual is required to pass certain examinations. He or she must also have considerable experience in the evaluating process.

The number of judges vary from level to level. It is fairly common to see two judges plus a head judge in each of the ten events at dual meets, which are competitions where two schools or clubs compete against each other. There are usually four judges plus a head judge at state meets and even more at the international and Olympic levels.

After each performance the judges note down their score, according to the established rules. The high and low scores are thrown out and the competitor's score is the average of the middle scores. Although the head judge does not actually submit a score, he or she carefully observes the entire process and mediates when there are differences of opinion.

There are three basic categories of competition:

COMPETITION 1A AND 1B: The team competitions plus preliminary compulsory and optional exercises.

COMPETITION II: The all-around finals. This is where the top gymnasts perform each of their respective events. The competitor with the highest point total is the all-around champion.

COMPETITION III: The individual event finals, with the top competitors from Competition 1A and 1B.

For their evaluations, the judges are guided by three general criteria in relation to the participant's performance: composition (called combination for men), execution, and degree of difficulty.

In regard to the composition or combination of the routine, the judges look at how the program is put together and must decide whether or not the gymnast has performed all the required elements. In judging the execution, the judges must determine how effectively the gymnast has executed his or her routine and how skillfully the various movements of the hands, back, arms, and legs were carried out.

The level-of-difficulty component is made up of A, B, and C factors, with A representing the least amount of difficulty and C the most. The greater the number of difficult moves the gymnast can execute effectively, the higher his or her score will be. In each routine, the competitor is required to have a certain number of A, B, and C elements.

At the outset of each event, the men are given a score of 9.4, the women 9.5. In order to get the "perfect 10," the routine must show originality, virtuosity, and a high degree of difficulty. Bonus points are awarded for well-executed movements, and deductions are given for not executing properly.

The judging of gymnastics is almost an art in itself, as it attempts to evaluate very subtle and intricate skills. There is almost always some controversy in the judging process. Judging in gymnastics is far more subjective than judging in most other individual and team sports.

5

RHYTHMIC GYMNASTICS

The traditional form of gymnastics is the type just described —the six men's and four women's events that have become standard in international competition.

A relatively new, and many think more beautiful, form of the sport for women only is rhythmic gymnastics. Although the roots of this sport also date back to ancient times, it first became a competitive event in Europe in 1962, with the first world championships held the following year. Traditionally, the Eastern bloc countries have been dominant in the sport; it only became popular in the United States recently.

In 1981 the International Olympic Committee designated rhythmic gymnastics as a full-fledged Olympic sport. Individual competitions were held at the 1984 Olympics in Los Angeles. In 1988, at the games in Seoul, Korea, group competition will be introduced. In group competition, routines are choreographed for six gymnasts performing simultaneously.

Rhythmic gymnastics involves the skills of gymnastics, acrobatics, dance, and even juggling. The gymnast combines flowing body movements with the handling of five different items: a rope (the size of a jump rope); a hoop (similar to a hula hoop); a ball (slightly larger than a softball); clubs (skinny bowling pins); and sticks with a colored ribbon on the end. Each routine is accompanied by music from a single instrument, usually a piano. The gymnast performs sixty to ninety seconds (two and a half to three minutes in the group exercises) on a 40-by-40-foot (12-by-12-m) mat, similar to the one used in the floor exercise routine, or a carpet or wooden floor of the same dimensions.

There are some distinctive movements associated with each of the five items:

ROPE—The gymnast skips, leaps, and jumps while performing swinging, circling, and figure-eight–type movements with the rope.

HOOP—The gymnast throws and catches the hoop while performing different body movements. The most interesting aspects here are the high tosses and varied body movements while attempting to catch the hoop.

BALL—Here, the gymnast performs a routine while balancing, tossing, rolling, and catching the ball.

CLUBS—The gymnast does various movements while throwing the clubs in the air, passing them behind the back, or juggling them.

RIBBONS—The routine is performed while the gymnast utilizes spiral, swinging, circling, and tossing motions with the ribbon.

One major difference between artistic and rhythmic gymnastics is the fact that flips, handstands, roundoffs, walkovers, and aerials are not allowed in rhythmic competition.

Rhythmic gymnastics performed with a ball, clubs, and ribbons

For rhythmic events there are four acting judges and a head judge, who is called upon to mediate any differences of opinion. The judges may award a maximum score of 10. The choreography is evaluated by how effectively the entire floor surface is used and how smoothly the equipment is handled. In each event, the gymnast must include eight elements, two of superior difficulty and six of medium difficulty. In the hoop, ball, and ribbon events, three of the elements must be performed with the nondominant hand. As in artistic gymnastics, there is an all-around competition as well as the individual events.

6

HOW TO BECOME
A GYMNAST

How do you become a gymnast? What inner qualities and basic skills do you need to succeed? How do you find the best instruction? What equipment is needed? How long does it take to become a competitive gymnast? These are just a few of the questions you must have if you are thinking of becoming involved in the sport.

The first step you should take after you decide to pursue gymnastics is to enroll in a proper program. Take your time choosing one. Contact the U.S. Gymnastics Federation, call your local recreations department, YMCA or YWCA, look in the telephone book under Gymnastics Schools, or ask your friends if they know of a good program. If the school is affiliated with the USGF, you know that it follows the time-honored philosophies of the organization.

It is generally acknowledged that the age of eight or nine is the right age for a youngster to begin participating in competitive gymnastics. Before that, a gymnast should concentrate on learning the basic skills or take dance classes to prepare for a more intense regimen later.

Here are some important points to keep in mind as you contemplate entering the world of gymnastics:

GETTING THE PROPER INSTRUCTION. By thoroughly researching the schools in your area, you should be able to find a school that has qualified instructors, experienced at all levels of coaching. Even though you do not yet know your abilities at this stage, it is still important that you benefit from the program. In the course of instruction you will be taught many things. These include basic gymnastic skills, such as handsprings and somersaults; the importance of positive mental attitude; discipline and creativity; and the development of the body in terms of strength, flexibility, rhythm, and stamina. Remember that there can be substantial cost involved in a gymnastics program. Obviously you and your parents need to discuss what the family budget can handle.

SAFETY. Like other forms of athletic activity, there is always a chance of injury. The school you select should have:

- spotting, which is having another person there to catch you in case of a fall.
- a properly lighted and padded gym.
- a high level of supervision.

Spotting, which is the practice of always having someone there to catch you in case of a fall, is an important safety feature of gymnastics classes.

- proper progressions; this means that the basic skills should be mastered before moving on to more difficult ones.
- proper equipment.
- instructors with a background in first aid.
- sufficient warm-up exercises.
- the monitoring of dietary habits.

PRACTICE. Practice, practice, and more practice is important to the gymnast. Be sure that the school you choose will give you the personalized instruction and time you need to develop your skills. Never attempt to learn any new skills without supervision by a qualified instructor and the proper equipment.

EQUIPMENT. In the beginning stages, equipment for the gymnast is minimal—leotards and gymnastics slippers (footies) or bare feet for the girls; gym shorts, T-shirts, and white athletic socks for the boys. As the gymnast progresses, such specialized equipment as handguards, wristbands, gymnastics shoes, and a more official uniform will be necessary.

Don't expect to become a Kurt Thomas or a Mary Lou Retton overnight. Every sport takes patience and hard work. Gymnastics, with its precise skills, is no exception. But with the proper instruction and a real effort on your part, it should certainly be possible for you to reach your goals.

Keep abreast of the gymnastics world by reading magazines and books on the sport and watching competitive gymnasts on television and in person. All these things will only add to your overall knowledge.

These tips should help get you started on the road to becoming a gymnast. For more specific information, including the names of gymnastics clubs near your home, write the U.S. Gymnastics Federation, Pan Am Plaza, Suite 300, 201 S. Capitol, Indianapolis, IN 46225, or call 317-237-5050.

7

THE GREATS OF GYMNASTICS

There have been numerous men and women over the years who have made substantial contributions to the sport of gymnastics. American gymnastics pioneers include Frank Cumiskey, a three-time Olympian who went on to become a judge at the sport's premier events; Jackie Fie, a female Olympic gymnast in 1956 who became a judge, official, lecturer, and teacher; and Bud Marquette, a gymnastics coach for half a century and founder of the first private gymnastics club in the United States, the Southern California Acro Team (SCATS).

In addition to these pioneers and many others around the world, there are a select few who have been closely associated with the sport's rise in popularity during the past two decades. Here's a closer look at these legends:

OLGA KORBUT

Although very few realized it at the time, Olga Korbut's performance at the 1972 Summer Olympics in Munich would become one of the landmark events in the sport's history. And, ironically, the entire experience would not have happened if Korbut hadn't stepped in for an injured teammate at the last moment.

Olga, then seventeen years old and from the Soviet Union, captured the hearts of those in Munich, and those watching on television, with her winning smile and remarkable gymnastic ability. She not only won three gold medals (two individual and one team) and one silver but also prompted a boom in gymnastics popularity around the globe, as boys and girls everywhere set their sights on becoming the next great Olympic champion. This was quite an accomplishment for a young girl who, only a few years before, had been deeply troubled by the fact that she was the shortest child in her class.

Olga's impact did not end in Munich. Following the Olympic Games, she continued her reign as the queen of gymnastics by becoming one of the sport's leading spokespeople. She made several trips of goodwill to the United States and as a result recruited more and more young people into the gymnastics world.

In 1976, Olga was again expected to be the darling of the Olympic Games, held in Montreal, Canada. But, as fate would have it, a young Rumanian (see below) would steal the show. Olga's accomplishments, however, were already a matter of record. She will always stand as one of the most influential gymnasts of all time.

NADIA COMANECI

The rise in gymnastics popularity was well under way by 1976, but the unbelievable effort by fourteen-year-old Nadia Comaneci (pronounced koh-mah-NEECH) at the Olympics that year in Montreal furthered the momentum.

Nadia was discovered by coach Bela Karolyi at the age of six in her hometown of Onesti (now Gheorghe Gheorghiu-Dej), Rumania. She was an established world-class competi-

Nadia Comaneci flies out of the uneven parallel bars into a perfect 10 score at the 1976 Olympics. It was the first perfect 10 in Olympic history.

tor by 1976 and even won the 1975 European all-around title. Nevertheless, her performance in Montreal stunned everyone, as she displayed an amazing mastery of both the technical and creative aspects of her routines. She made enormously difficult movements look easy.

Although she wore a more detached look on her face than the effervescent Olga did, Nadia enthralled the crowd the same way Olga had done four years earlier. Not only did she dominate the competition with three gold medals, a silver, and a bronze, she also recorded the first "perfect 10s" in Olympic history. She received these for her performances on the balance beam and uneven parallel bars, finishing with seven perfect scores. Four years later, at the Olympics in Moscow, the eighteen-year-old Nadia proved she still had that special touch, as she captured two more gold medals to add to her collection.

"She is the epitome of perfection," said one U.S. official at the time. "She has everything going for her—mind, body, discipline, coach, facilities, flexibility, strength, speed, endurance, and the ability to block out the whole world."

Nadia is still very active in gymnastics, serving as a coach and a judge in her native country.

CATHY RIGBY

The decade of the 1970s was a very special time for gymnastics, and, as we have seen, it was two teenagers from foreign lands who had the greatest impact on gymnastics in the United States. However, before Korbut and Comaneci came

Kathy Rigby is all concentration as she trains for the 1972 Olympics.

onto the scene, there was a very talented girl from California who gave young Americans the hope that someday they, too, could excel at the international level. Her name was Cathy Rigby.

Cathy did not achieve the same kind of Olympic success as Korbut and Comaneci. Still, she joins them in that elite circle of gymnasts who have made extraordinary contributions to the sport. Exceptional skills, a fiery competitive spirit, and an engaging personality were her trademarks.

Cathy's gymnastic training began with Bud Marquette's SCATS in Long Beach, California, at the age of ten. She became the youngest member of the U.S. Olympic gymnastics team five years later (1968) and placed a respectable sixteenth. This was the highest finish ever for an American female gymnast up to that time.

In 1970, Cathy established herself as the first American to win a medal at the world championship level, with a silver at the world meet in Yugoslavia. In 1972, she returned to Olympic competition with a fine tenth-place finish. By the time she was through competing, in 1972, Rigby had won twelve medals in international competition, including eight golds, and was ranked number five in the world in women's gymnastics.

Cathy has continued to be active in gymnastics. She is a gymnastics commentator for ABC-TV and has set up her own gymnastics academies.

MARY LOU RETTON

Following in the footsteps of Korbut, Comaneci, and Rigby, Mary Lou Retton became the sweetheart of the 1984 Olympics in Los Angeles. She captured the gold medal in the all-around competition—a first for an American—plus a silver and two bronzes in the individual apparatus events.

Retton was coached by the same Bela Karolyi who had

tutored Nadia Comaneci before he moved to the United States. She revolutionized the sport with her power, speed, energy, and agility. Standing at just 4 feet 9 inches (1.4 m), the sixteen-year-old from West Virginia with a wide smile and determined nature, emerged from the games as the sport's dominant figure the way Olga and Nadia did in the seventies.

Retton's career began when her mother, out of sheer desperation, enrolled her in a dance and acrobatics class. "I was one of those hyper kids, always jumping up and down on the couch and breaking things," Mary Lou said. Her skills continued to improve, and the rest is history.

In addition to Mary Lou's enormous personal achievements, she became the leader of the 1984 women's U.S. gymnastics team, which set a new standard for American success in the Olympics. With such outstanding talents as Retton, Julianne McNamara, Kathy Johnson, and Tracee Talavera, the squad won a silver in the team competition. They narrowly missed defeating the Rumanians for the gold.

Since the 1984 games, Mary Lou has become a media celebrity. She has appeared in numerous TV commercials, has worked as a gymnastics commentator for NBC-TV, and has made a variety of personal appearances while attending the University of Texas as a student, majoring in communications.

Whatever the future has in store for Mary Lou Retton, she will always have a special place in American gymnastics history. She was the first American to win an Olympic all-around gold medal and was a member of the finest women's gymnastics team in the country's history.

"She's so powerful physically and she's mentally prepared, too," Karolyi said of Mary Lou. "I was teaching gymnastics twenty-five years and I had many world and Olympic champions, but I never had somebody more positive and dedicated than this little girl."

KURT THOMAS

It seems as if the women have had the most impact in gymnastics during the past couple of decades, but there have also been many outstanding men who have made their marks in the sport. Perhaps the greatest American performer was Kurt Thomas. Thomas brought respectability to male gymnastics in the United States.

A product of Indiana State University, Thomas captured more than a dozen titles in his career. At the 1978 world championships in France, he became the first American to win an individual gold medal at the "Worlds." In 1979, at the world championships, he won the gold for both the floor exercise and horizontal bar and won a silver in the all-around. The high point for Thomas had to be the day he was presented the Sullivan Award as the nation's premier amateur athlete for 1979.

Kurt was never able to prove himself in Olympic competition. He would have been a leading candidate to win a gold medal in 1980, but the Americans boycotted the games in Moscow that year for political reasons. With that went Kurt's hopes.

Kurt Thomas will long be remembered for his exceptional gymnastic accomplishments. Among them was his introduction of the "Thomas flair," an innovative routine used on the pommel horse and parallel bars and in the floor exercise.

1984 U.S. MEN'S
OLYMPIC GYMNASTICS TEAM

The legacy of excellence that Kurt Thomas left the U.S. men's gymnastics program was realized in 1984. This was when the U.S. men's team emerged from the Olympics in Los Angeles as the best team in the world.

The American team gold medal victory in Los Angeles was over outstanding teams from China and Japan. It was the Summer Olympics equivalent to the U.S. Olympic hockey team's surprising gold medal triumph at the 1980 winter games in Lake Placid. Long considered the "poor cousins" of international gymnastics, the United States finally arrived after years of building a program of respectability. "I never thought I'd see this happen in my lifetime," said U.S. coach Abie Grossfeld. "No one who knows gymnastics thought we'd beat the Chinese. . . . No one thought we would do it."

Although the triumph was a team effort, the squad was comprised of some of the finest American gymnasts ever, who combined their individual skills to capture the gold.

The victorious U.S. men's gymnastics team at the 1984 Olympic Games. Bart Conner (left) and Peter Vidmar stand together with their arms raised in triumph.

The elder statesman of the team was Bart Conner, who along with Kurt Thomas constituted the heart of the U.S. hopes in the 1970s. After a devastating injury, Conner fought back to compete in Los Angeles and captured an individual gold medal on the parallel bars in addition to his team's gold.

Peter Vidmar from UCLA had been on the U.S. national team since 1978. Like Thomas and Conner he missed out in 1980 because of the boycott. At Los Angeles, Vidmar tied for the gold in the pommel horse and won a silver in the all-around.

Vidmar's UCLA teammate, Mitch Gaylord, won three bronze medals—on the rings, vault (tie), and parallel bars. He made his innovative horizontal bar routine, the "Gaylord II," a national craze.

Other team members who contributed substantially to the gold medal were UCLA's Tim Daggett, who should be a top U.S. hope in the 1988 Olympics, and James Hartung and Scott Johnson, both products of the University of Nebraska.

The U.S. men's accomplishment in 1984 had an enormous impact at home. As Vidmar said at the time, "We made history for the United States today. It's a whole new era for men's gymnastics in the United States."

8

THE 1988
SUMMER OLYMPICS

With the 1988 Summer Olympics upon us, many are asking, who will make up the next wave of gymnasts to capture the attention of America and the world?

At the time of this writing it was not known for sure who would participate, nor who would emerge as the new stars of the sport. But it is safe to assume that the Soviet Union, Japan, China, Rumania, and the United States would be among the top teams when the Olympics commenced in Seoul, Korea. Following is a look at some of the individual hopefuls.

KRISTIE PHILLIPS, PHOEBE MILLS,
UNITED STATES

The similarities between Kristie Phillips and Mary Lou Retton were noted years ago. Not only do the two share the distinction of having learned from the same coach (Bela Karolyi), they both also have vibrant personalities. Kristie, however, has tried to establish her own identity.

"I guess it's good exposure for me to be Mary Lou Number 2," she said at the age of fourteen in 1986. "But I'd rather be Kristie Number 1."

At four years old, Kristie watched as Nadia Comaneci excelled at the Montreal Olympics. Shortly after, she began participating in the sport. By the time she was eight, she was aiming for the 1988 Olympic Games.

Kristie began working with Karolyi in Houston, Texas, when she was ten. A native of Baton Rouge, Louisiana, she went to Atlanta to train for two years and in 1984 returned to Karolyi's school in Houston as a much-improved athlete.

In her first major competition, the highly competitive 1986 American Cup, Kristie emerged as the top woman in the all-around. This was the same title Mary Lou had captured in 1983, setting the stage for her Olympic success.

Perhaps Mary Lou Retton herself said it best when she made the following observation in 1986: "When I met Kristie three years ago, I saw she had a personality sort of like mine—outgoing, a big smile. I said to myself, 'this girl is going to make it.'"

A friend and rival of Kristie Phillips, Phoebe Mills is also a product of Bela Karolyi's gymnastics school. And like Kristie, Phoebe is shooting for the gold at Seoul.

"I think I have as good a chance as Mary Lou Retton ever did to go to the Olympics and win the gold," said the fourteen-year-old Phoebe in 1986. This was shortly after she gained the spotlight by winning the gold medal in the all-around plus three individual golds at a U.S.–China meet. "My confidence is growing gradually," she added.

Although Phoebe—like Kristie—hopes to duplicate Mary Lou's success, she also has the utmost respect for the 1984 Olympic sweetheart. "I envy Mary Lou and what she has done," Phoebe said. "She has given me a lot of inspiration."

Kristie Phillips (left) and Phoebe Mills

ELENA SHOUSHOUNOVA,
IRINA BARAKSANOVA,
AND VERA KOLESNIKOVA,
SOVIET UNION

A native of Leningrad, Elena Shoushounova has been a member of the Soviet national team since 1983. A versatile gymnast who will be sixteen years old in 1988, she is a past world champion in the all-around.

An outstanding performer on all four apparatus, Irina Baraksanova, from the town of Tashkent, has set her sights on the gold. And, like Kristie Phillips and Phoebe Mills, she is trying to develop her own identity.

"I very much love gymnastics and I love performing," she has said. "I idolize Olga Korbut, but I feel no pressure to be the next Olga. I just want to be one of the top gymnasts— one of the (best) in my country." She will be nineteen in 1988.

Vera Kolesnikova, who will be twenty in 1988, is from the town of Voronezh. A national team member since 1983, she won the gold medal in the all-around and balance beam at the 1986 Goodwill Games and had a silver in the uneven parallel bars.

AUGUSTINA BADEA,
DANIELA SILIVAS, AND
CAMELIA VOINEA, RUMANIA

These three teenage girls are among the top Rumanian gymnasts.

Top left: *Elena Shoushounova.* Bottom left: *Daniela Silivas.* Top to bottom right: *Irina Baraksanova, Oksana Omelianchik (from the USSR), and Augustina Badea.*

YURI KOROLEV, VALENTIN MOGILNY, AND
VALERI LJUKIN, SOVIET UNION

A past world champion in the all-around and perhaps the finest male gymnast of the early 1980s, Korolev is from the town of Vladimir. He will be twenty-six in 1988.

A native of Moscow who will be twenty-three in 1988, Mogilny is one of the most outstanding Soviet gymnasts. He won gold medals in the pommel horse, parallel bars, and rings at the 1986 Goodwill Games and captured silver medals in the floor exercise and all-around.

One of the most innovative gymnasts in the floor exercise, Valeri Ljukin won the 1987 European championship in that event. He will be twenty-two in 1988.

Yuri Korolev

Li Ning

LI NING,
CHINA

One of the elder statesmen of men's gymnastics and a bona fide Olympic champion, Ning captured gold medals in the floor exercise, pommel horse (tie), and rings (tie) at the 1984 games in Los Angeles. He also won a silver medal in the vault event and a bronze in the all-around.

SYLVIO KROLL,
EAST GERMANY

Kroll, a native of Lubben, is a versatile performer who was the 1985 world champion in the parallel bars and a gold medalist in the vault at the 1986 World Cup. He will be twenty-three in 1988.

TIM DAGGETT,
SCOTT JOHNSON, AND
BRIAN GINSBERG, UNITED STATES

A key member of the 1984 gold medal-winning U.S. squad, Daggett is a past U.S. national all-around champion. He will be a top American hope if he recovers from a 1987 neck injury and more serious leg injury. He is from West Springfield, Massachusetts, and will be twenty-five in 1988.

Now living in Lincoln, Nebraska, Scott Johnson was a member of the gold medal-winning American team in 1984 and has been a member of the U.S. national squad since 1981. Johnson, who will be twenty-seven in 1988, captured the U.S. and Pan American Games men's all-around titles in 1987.

A member of the U.S. national team since 1985, Ginsberg was the gold medal winner in the all-around at the 1987 American Cup. He won an individual gold in the floor exercise, tied for top honors with Scott Johnson in the pommel horse and rings, and won a silver in the horizontal bar event. Ginsberg, who lives in Los Angeles, will be twenty-two in 1988.

MARINA KUNYAVSKY, DIANE SIMPSON,
UNITED STATES

In the rhythmic gymnastics arena, the Bulgarians and Soviets should be among the best overall teams. However, the United States has two of the top competitors—past

Above: *Tim Daggett*
Below: *Scott Johnson (left)*
and Brian Ginsberg

national champion Marina Kunyavsky of Los Angeles and Diane Simpson of Evanston, Illinois.

Born in Leningrad in the Soviet Union, Marina began training in 1975 and has been on the U.S. national team since 1982. She will be twenty-three in 1988.

"Energy generated into the air as Kunyavsky took to the floor. Kunyavsky demonstrated why she is our country's best," it was written after one of Marina's performances. "Besides having great expression, she possesses incredible technical ability . . ."

As an eighteen-year-old in 1987, Diane won two gold and two silver medals at the Pan American Games. This included a silver in the all-around.

All of these gifted athletes, and many others from countries around the world, will be in Korea aiming for the ultimate in gymnastics—the distinction of being an Olympic champion.

CURRENT USGF
MEMBER ORGANIZATIONS

Amateur Athletic Union
3400 W. 86th Street
Indianapolis, IN 46268

American Turners
c/o 11624 E. 25th
Independence, MO 64052

Junior Boys Gymnastics Coaches Association
140 N. Louise
Glendale, CA 91206
(c/o Rich Boccia)

National Association for Girls and Women in Sports
c/o Dr. Mimi Murray
Springfield College
Springfield, MA 01109

National Association of Collegiate Gymnastics
    Coaches—Men
RR 2, Box 233
Iowa City, IA 52240

National Association of Collegiate Gymnastics
    Coaches—Women
c/o Judy Avener
Penn State Lady Lions
White Building
University Park, PA 16802

National Association of Intercollegiate Athletics
1221 Baltimore
Kansas City, MO 64105

National Association of Womens Gymnastics
    Judges
c/o 4761 N. Barton
Fresno, CA 93726

National Collegiate Athletic Association
    (NCAA)
P.O. Box 1906
Mission, KS 66201

National Federation of State High School
    Association
11724 Plaza Circle
Kansas City, MO 64195

National Gymnastics Judges Association
c/o Mike Milidonis
1476 Kirtland
Ann Arbor, MI 48103

National High School Gymnastics
    Coaches Association
567 S. LaSalle Street
Des Plaines, IL 60016

National Jewish Welfare Board
331 Aspen Lane
Highland Park, IL 60035

Rhythmic Gymnastics Coaches Association
c/o 929 Barhugh Place
San Pedro, CA 90731

Special Olympics, Inc.
International Headquarters
1350 New York Avenue, #500
Washington, DC 20005

United States Association of Independent
    Gymnastics Clubs
235 Pinehurst Road
Wilmington, DE 19803

United States Elite Coaches Association—
    Men
c/o Jim Howard
Athletic Department
University of Nebraska
Lincoln, NE 68583

United States Elite Coaches Association—
    Women
c/o Roe Kreutzer
8232 Vista Drive
Scottsdale, AZ 85253

United States Sports Acrobatics Federation
Dr. Joseph Schabacker, President
5538 S. Marine Drive
Tempe, AZ 85283

USGF National Womens Program Committee
5653 W. 71st Circle
Arvada, CO 80003

YMCA of the USA
101 N. Wacker Drive
Chicago, IL 60606

INDEX

Page numbers in italics refer to illustrations

Acrobatic elements, 23
Amplitude, 23
Arch, 23
Artistic gymnastics, 22–58
    judging and scoring of, 56–58
    men's events in, 40–55
    terms used in, 23–27
    women's events in, 28–39

Backward rolls, 23
Badea, Augustina, 80, *81*
Balance beam, 35–37
Ball movements, 60, *61*

Baraksanova, Irina, 80, *81*
Blind releases, 23
Body waves, 23
Boutard, Michel, *49*
Bridges, 23

Cartwheels, 24, 39
Casts, 24, 34
Clubs, 60, *61*
Comaneci, Nadia, 16, *17*, 68–70, 73, 78
Competitions, 19–20, 22, 57
Conner, Bart, *75*, 76
Cumiskey, Frank, 67

Daggett, Tim, 76, 84, *85*
Degree of difficulty, 57
Diamidov turn, 53
Dismounts, 24

Equipment, 66

Federation of International
    Gymnastics (FIG), 19, 36,
    39, 56
Fie, Jackie, 67
Flip-flops (flic-flacs), 24
Floor exercise
    for men, 40–41
    for women, 37–39
Forward rolls, 24
Frederick, Marcia, 16, 19

Gaylord, Mitch, 76
Germany, 14
Giant swings, 24, 34, 46, 54
Ginsberg, Brian, 84, *85*
Greece, ancient, 12–13
Grossfeld, Abie, 75
Gymnasia, 12, *13*

Handsprings, 26, 30
Hartung, James, 76
Headsprings, 26
Hip circles, 26, 34
Hoop movements, 60
Horizontal bar, *52*, 54–55
Hurdles, 26

Jahn, Frederick, 14
Johnson, Kathy, *25*, 73
Johnson, Scott, 76, 84, *85*
Judging, 56–58, 62

Karolyi, Bela, 68, 72–73, 77,
    78
Kasamatsu vault, 51
Kips, 26
Kolesnikova, Vera, 80
Korbut, Olga, 16, *17*, 67–68,
    70, 80
Kormann, Peter, 16, 19
Korolev, Yuri, 82
Kroll, Sylvio, 83
Kunyavsky, Marina, 86

Lakes, Charlie, *52*
Layouts, 26
Li Ning, 83
Ljukin, Valeri, 82

McNamara, Julianne, 73
Marquette, Bud, 67, 72
Men's events, 40–55
    floor exercise, 40–41
    horizontal bar, *52*, 54–55
    parallel bars, 51–53
    pommel horse, 42–44
    rings, 44–46
    vault, 49–51
Mills, Phoebe, 77, 78, *79*
Mogilny, Valentin, 82
Muths, Johann Guts, 14

Olympic Games, 14, 22, 59
    gymnastic greats at,
        67–76

Olympic Games
(continued)
    origins of, 12–13
    summer 1988, 77–86
    U.S. medalists at, 16–19,
       70–76
Omelianchik, Oksana, *81*

Parallel bars, 51–53
Phillips, Kristie, 77–78, *79*
Pikes, 26
Pirouettes, 26
Pommel horse, 13, 42–44
Practice, 66

Retton, Mary Lou, *18*, 19,
   72–73, 77–78
Rhythmic gymnastics, 22,
   59–62, 86
Ribbons, 60, *61*
Rigby, Cathy, 16, 19, 70–72
Rings, 44–46
Roman empire, 12, 13
Rope movements, 60
Roundoffs, 26

Safety measures, 64–66
Saltos, 26, 39
Schlesinger, Tom, *45*
Scissors, *43*, 44
Scoring, 56–58, 62
Shoushounova, Elena, 80, *81*
Silivas, Daniela, 80, *81*

Simpson, Diane, 86
Spotting, 64, *65*
Squats, 27
Sticking, 27
Straddles, 27

Talavera, Tracee, 73
Thomas, Kurt, 16, *18*, 19, 44,
   74, 76
Tsukahara vault, 30–31, 51,
   61
Tucks, 27
Twists, 27

Uneven parallel bars, 31–34
U.S. Gymnastics Federation
   (USGF), 19–20, 66, 87–90

Vault, 13
    for men, 49–51
    for women, 28–31
Vidmar, Peter, *75*, 76
Virtuosity, 27
Voinea, Camelia, 80

Walkovers, 27
Women's events, 28–39
    balance beam, 35–37
    floor exercise, 37–39
    uneven parallel bars,
      31–34
    vault, 28–31

ABOUT THE AUTHOR

Art Berke is currently the Director of Sports and Prime Time Sales Development for the ABC television network. From 1980 to 1984 he was the primary publicist for such ABC sports series as "Wide World of Sports," "Monday Night Football," and Howard Cosell's "ABC SportsBeat," and was a member of the ABC team for both the 1984 Winter and Summer Olympic Games. Prior to joining the network, Art was associate director of information, in charge of publications, for the baseball commissioner's office.

Art has written three previous books—*Unsung Heroes of the Major Leagues* (Random House, 1976), *This Date in Chicago White Sox History* (Stein & Day, 1982), and *ABC Sports: The First Twenty-Five Years* (ABC Television, 1985)—and served as editor in chief of *The Lincoln Library of Sports Champions,* a fourteen-volume encyclopedia. He is also the author of *Babe Ruth,* soon to be published by Franklin Watts. Art and his wife, Bonnie, reside in Harmon Cove, New Jersey.